CUTE CHRISTMAS COLORING BOOK FOR KIDS

50 awesome Christmas-themed illustrations to colorize & have fun

Have Fun

find our Christmas Nutcracker-Ballet apparel here
https://shop.diothena.design/shop

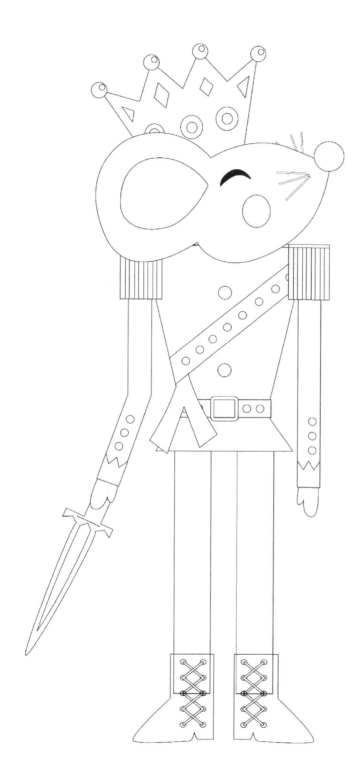

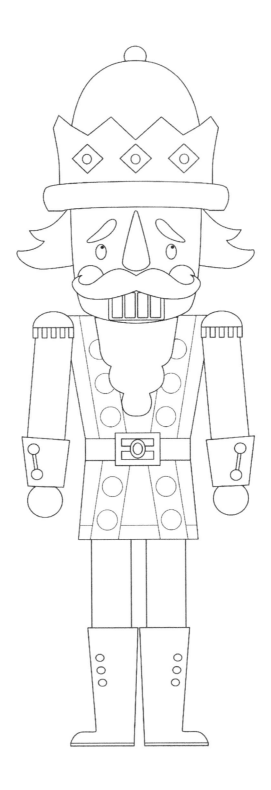

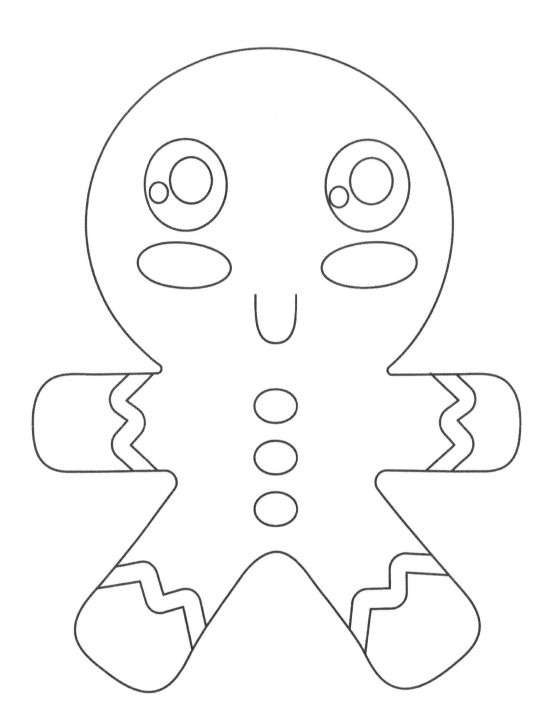

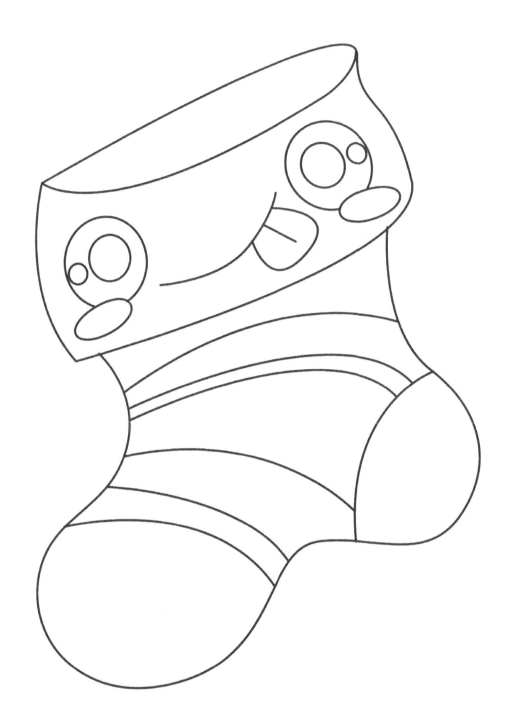

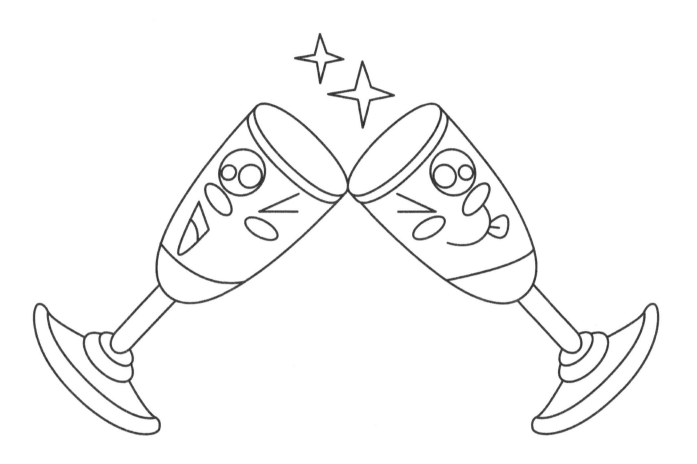

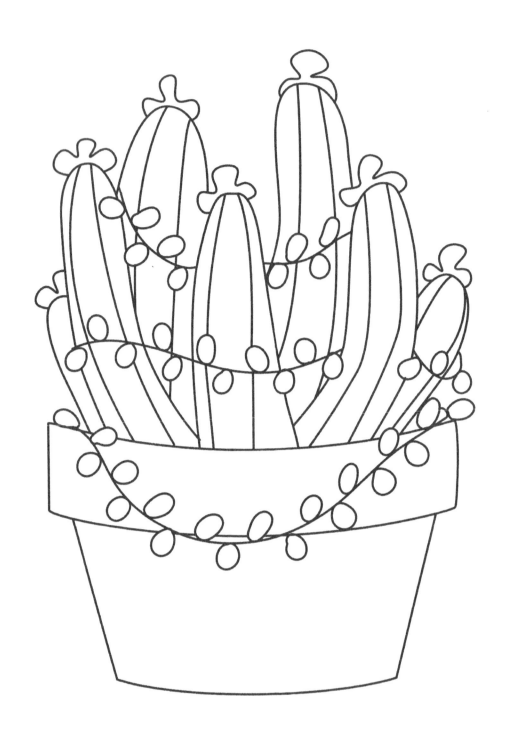

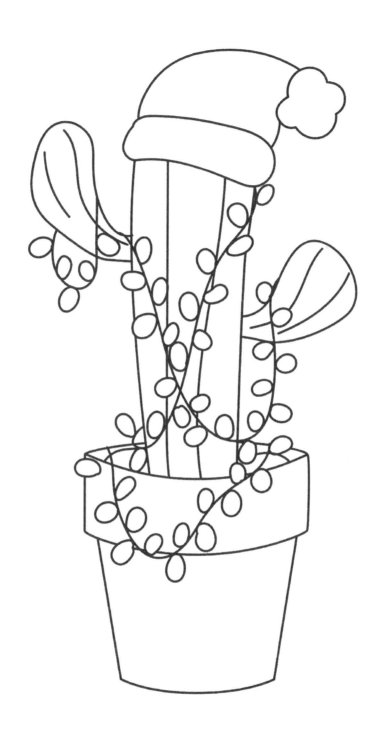

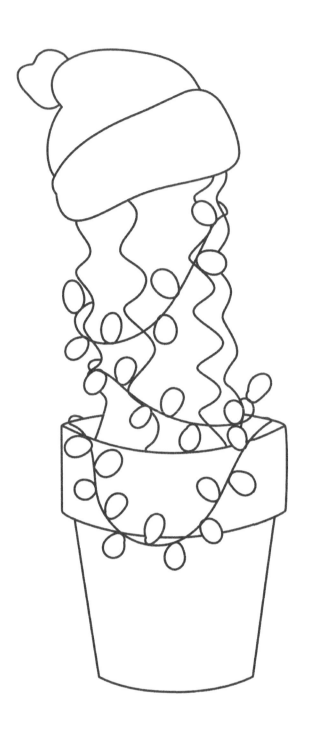

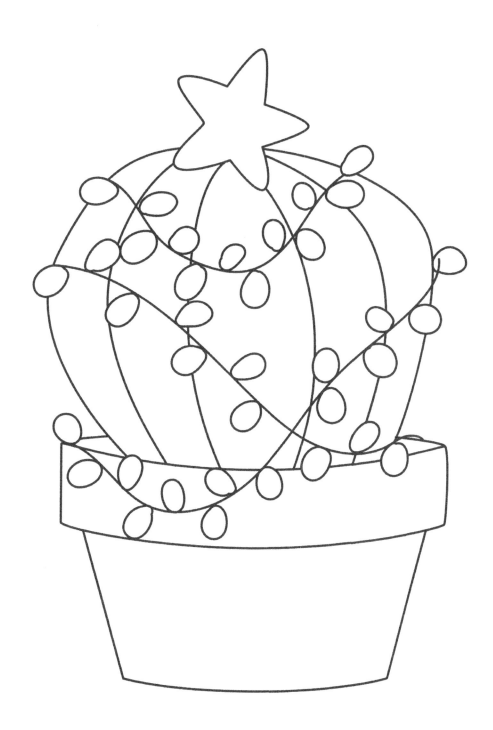

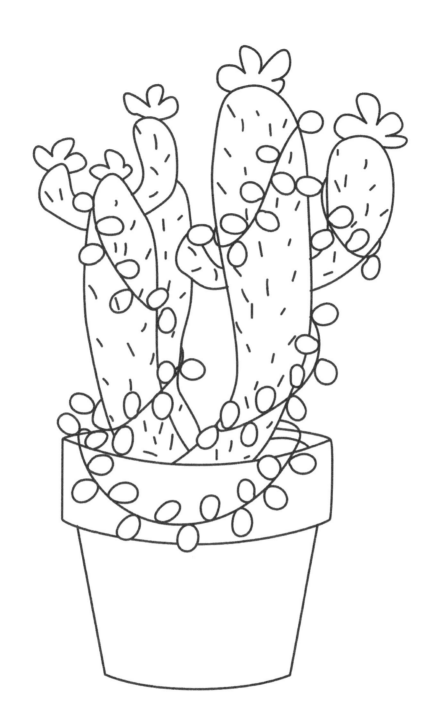

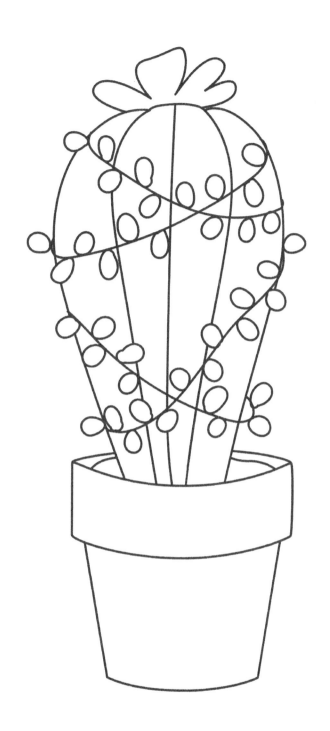

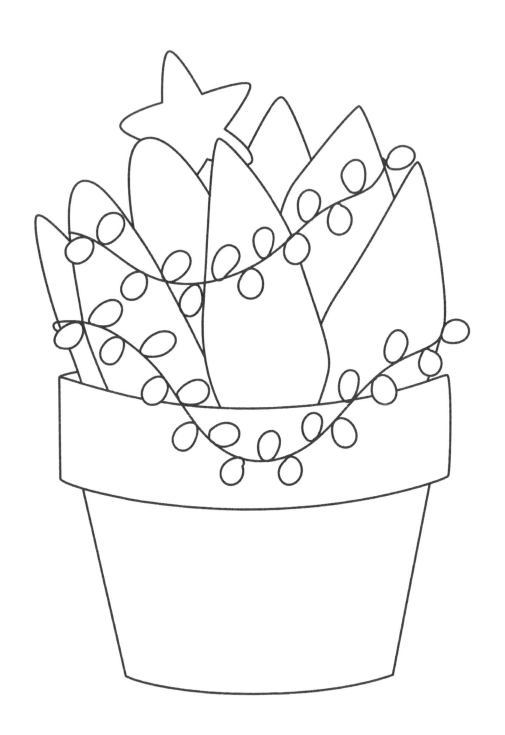

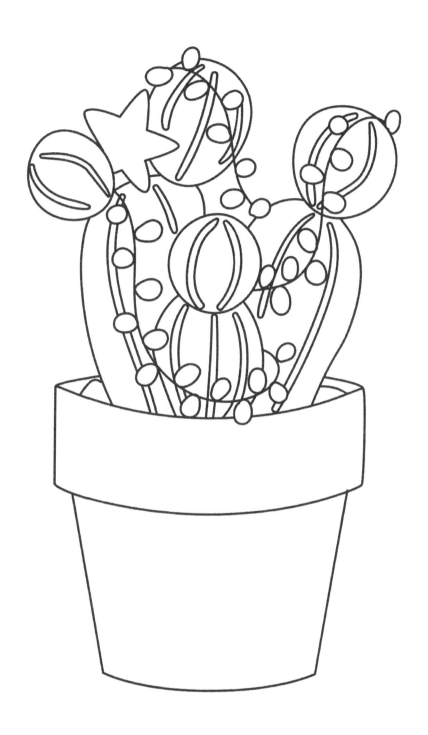

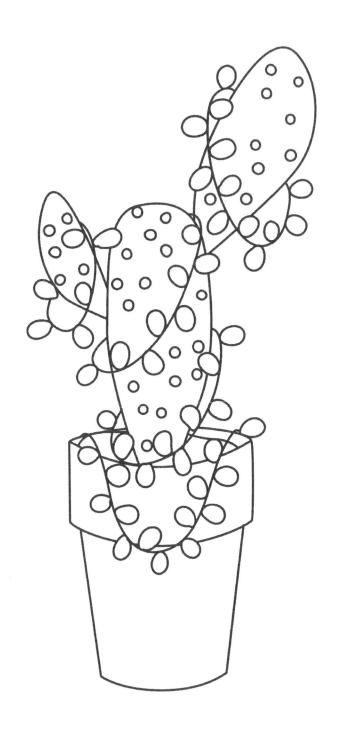

Find our Christmas Nutcracker Ballet apparel here:

https://shop.diothena.design/shop

Dedicated to Leni & Elias

Made in the USA
Las Vegas, NV
07 December 2023

82253686R10031